Hernando de Soto

A Proud Heritage The Hispanic Library

Hernando de Soto

A Life of Adventure

R. Conrad Stein

Content Adviser: John Kessell, PhD
Professor Emeritus
University of New Mexico
Albuquerque, New Mexico

Published in the United States of America by The Child's World®
PO Box 326 • Chanhassen, MN 55317-0326 • 800-599-READ • www.childsworld.com

Acknowledgments
   The Child's World®: Mary Berendes, Publishing Director

   Editorial Directions, Inc.: E. Russell Primm, Editorial Director; Pam Rosenberg, Project
   Editor; Katie Marsico, Associate Editor; Matt Messbarger, Editorial Assistant; Susan Hindman,
   Copyeditor; Lucia Raatma, Proofreader; Judith Frisbie, Fact Checker; Timothy Griffin/
   IndexServ, Indexer; Dawn Friedman, Photo Researcher; Linda S. Koutris, Photo Selector

   The Creative Spark: Mary Francis and Rob Court, Design and Page Production

   XNR Productions, Inc.: Cartography

Photos
   Cover: Hernando de Soto discovers the Mississippi River, 19th century engraving, The
   Granger Collection, New York

   Giraudon /Art Resource, NY: 9; Bildarchiv Preussischer Kulturbesitz/Art Resource, NY: 23,
   25; Réunion des Musées Nationaux/Art Resource, NY: 27; Bertrand Rieger/Museart/Corbis
   Sygma: 7; Bob Krist/Corbis: 13; Archivo Iconografico, S.A./Corbis: 17; Brian A. Vikander/
   Corbis: 20; Graham Neden, Ecoscene/Corbis: 22; Richard Cummins/Corbis: 31; Florida State
   Archives: 34; The Granger Collection, New York: 8, 10, 11, 21, 29; Hulton I Archive/Getty
   Images: 30; North Wind Picture Archives: 14, 15, 18, 24, 26, 35, 36; Stock Montage, Inc.: 19.

Library of Congress Cataloging-in-Publication Data
   Stein, R. Conrad.
      Hernando de Soto : a life of adventure / by R. Conrad Stein.
         p. cm. — (A proud heritage)
      Includes bibliographical references and index.
      ISBN 1-59296-385-4 (Library Bound : alk. paper) 1. Soto, Hernando de, ca. 1500–1542—
   Juvenile literature. 2. Explorers—America—Biography—Juvenile literature. 3. Explorers—
   Spain—Biography—Juvenile literature. 4. America—Discovery and exploration—Spanish—
   Juvenile literature. 5. Southern States—Discovery and exploration—Spanish—Juvenile
   literature. I. Title. II. Proud heritage (Child's World (Firm))
      E125.S7S83 2005
      970.01'6'092—dc22   2004018047

One	Birth of a Conqueror	6
Two	Joining the Great Adventure	12
Three	With Pizarro to the Land of the Incas	16
Four	Return to the Americas	28
	Timeline	37
	Glossary	38
	Further Information	39
	Index	40

Chapter One

Birth of a Conqueror

"Renew your courage, Amadís, for the hardest struggles still lie ahead in these dark lands."

(from *Amadís of Gaul,* the favorite book of Spanish explorer Hernando de Soto.)

Extremadura is a dry, dusty region in southwestern Spain. In the 1500s, the region held Spain's worst farmland. That is why young men from Extremadura often gave up farming to become soldiers. Many of these men joined the ranks of the conquistadores, the conquerors. They sailed to the newly discovered lands in the Americas, conquered the Native American people there, and colonized the land for Spain. In the Americas, the men from Extremadura banded together as if they belonged to a special club and helped one another advance in the conquistador ranks.

The Extremadura region of Spain was the birthplace of many of the conquistadores.

Without question, the Spanish conquistadores wrote a cruel chapter in world history. They killed thousands of Native Americans. However, the history books often overlook the fact that the conquistadores were magnificent explorers. The bold Spaniards marched into thick jungles, climbed rugged mountains, and sailed through unknown seas. One Spanish explorer who seemed to know no fear was Hernando de Soto.

Hernando de Soto was born in Jérez de los Caballeros in the Extremadura region of Spain.

De Soto was born in Extremadura in the year 1500 (some historians say his birth date was 1496). Little is known about his boyhood. His father must have had some wealth because it appears that Hernando attended school long enough to learn basic reading and writing. Like many other boys from his region, he dreamed of being a soldier. He probably played soldier games with his friends and used wooden swords for **mock** sword fights.

When he was a teenager, Hernando traveled to the port city of Seville. At the time, the countryside of Extremadura was alive with exciting news about magnificent discoveries on the other side of the Atlantic Ocean. According to the reports, land in the Americas was wild, beautiful, and dangerous. Most

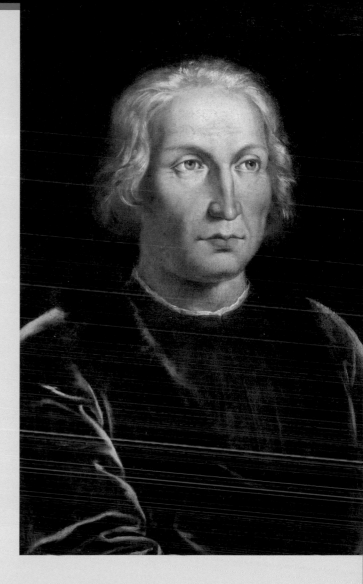

In 1492, Italian sea captain Christopher Columbus set sail to find a short route to the Indies. In those days, the Indies included the countries of India, China, and Japan. Columbus was on a mission for the Spanish king and queen. He hoped to reach the Indies by sailing west around the world. Instead of landing in the Indies, he discovered the vast continents of North America and South America. Because he thought he was in the Indies, he mistakenly called the people of the Americas "Indians." Spain moved quickly to build an empire in the Americas. By the early 1500s, Spain had started colonies on the island of Hispaniola (home to the modern-day nations of Haiti and the Dominican Republic) and on the island of Cuba.

The port city of Seville was the center of exploration and trade between Spain and the Americas in the 1500s.

important, what the Europeans considered a "New World" promised to bring riches to adventurous young men from Spain. It was even rumored that across the waters, gold was so common the people who lived there wore golden hats.

While in Seville, Hernando de Soto was interviewed by a 70-year-old army colonel named Pedro Arias de Ávila, who was called Pedrarias. Colonel

Pedrarias was feared throughout Spain for his violent temper. The aging colonel, however, took an instant liking to Hernando. The colonel was about to lead a fleet of ships across the Atlantic. His wife and two young daughters would accompany him on the voyage. He hired Hernando to look after them onboard ship and while they were in the Americas. During their travels, the wife and two daughters of Colonel Pedrarias grew fond of the young, handsome de Soto.

Caravels were a popular kind of sailing ship used by Spanish explorers in the 1500s.

Chapter Two

Joining the Great Adventure

In 1514, the fleet of ships commanded by Pedrarias stopped at Dominica Island. It was here that the teenage Hernando de Soto saw his first incident of conquistador cruelty. One young crew member decided to take a walk on the beach of this enchanting island. The young man was late coming back, and Colonel Pedrarias ordered him to be hung from a tree. De Soto learned why his boss, Pedrarias, was called the **Scourge** of God.

Even though he witnessed this cruelty, de Soto was determined to press on with his adventure. Like most conquistadores, he looked to the New World to fulfill his dreams. Spanish conquistadores sailed to the Americas driven by three ideals: God, gold, and glory. The Spaniards **fervently** believed it was their duty as Christians to bring Christianity to the Indians of the

The island of Dominica is located in the Caribbean Sea. It is about 29 miles (47 kilometers) long and 16 miles (26 km) across at its widest point.

Americas. The conquistadores also wanted to get rich. Wild stories were told about gold in the Americas being as common as pebbles on a Spanish beach. Finally, the conquistadores sought glory on the battlefield. Spain was a military society, and a man had to prove he was courageous in battle to gain respect.

The Pedrarias fleet next sailed to what is now the country of Colombia in South America. There Hernando de Soto had his first taste of battle. Soldiers under Pedrarias stormed through the countryside burning villages, grabbing whatever food they could find, and stealing gold trinkets. When the Native Americans fought back, they were slaughtered by superior Spanish weapons.

The people of Colombia had never seen guns, the "fire sticks" that killed at long range. Nor had they seen horses, the beasts that thundered into their ranks bearing sword-wielding soldiers. Young de Soto learned the power of Spanish arms. He saw how a few Spanish soldiers armed with iron swords and guns could defeat a large force of Indian warriors who fought with spears and arrows.

At a settlement near Colombia, de Soto met the remarkable explorer Vasco

SLAUGHTER OF THE XARAGUANS AND CAPTURE OF THEIR QUEEN.

Many Native Americans were killed when the Spanish conquistadores invaded South America.

Núñez de Balboa. In 1513, Balboa had been the first European to see the Pacific Ocean. Unlike many other Spaniards, Balboa was at times kind and respectful toward the Native Americans. De Soto and Balboa became friends. Both men were from the Extremadura region.

But de Soto noticed that his boss, Colonel Pedrarias, had no love for Balboa. The colonel was jealous because

Balboa claims the Pacific Ocean for Spain in 1513. Born in Extremadura in 1475, Balboa left Spain in 1501 to explore South America.

Balboa was gaining popularity in Spain. The aging colonel was hostile toward any Spaniard in the Americas who seemed to be gaining political power. In 1519, Pedrarias falsely accused Balboa of **treason** against the Spanish government. After a speedy trial, Balboa was beheaded in the village square at the Colombian settlement of Acla. Pedrarias, the Scourge of God, had struck again.

Chapter Three

With Pizarro to the Land of the Incas

De Soto was part of an exploring mission that **trekked** through the wilds of Panama. It was there that he discovered the thrill of seeing new lands and exotic creatures. Chattering monkeys watched the advancing party from the branches. Birds with bright green and orange feathers soared above jungle trails. The explorers saw their first alligator, which one European described as a "snake with legs." On the Pacific coast, a local chief told de Soto that a great nation lay to the south. "What is the name of that nation?" asked de Soto. The chief answered, "Birú." Spaniards would later call this place Peru, and it would be the site of one of de Soto's great adventures.

The conquistadores clung to the belief that somewhere in the huge American continent lived advanced civilizations whose people were rich in gold. But so far, the Spanish adventurers had found mostly muddy villages whose residents had nothing but a few tiny golden ornaments.

Then, in 1519, the conquistador Hernando Cortés discovered the Aztec capital deep in the mountains of Mexico. It was a city of tall pyramids and magnificent palaces. Best of all, Cortés and his men found the Aztec treasury—a fabulous collection of gold statues, sparkling emeralds, and other precious jewels.

Rumors persisted that enormous wealth could be found to the south, along the Pacific

Hernando Cortés discovered the Aztec capital of Tenochtitlán in 1519. In 1521, he succeeded in conquering the Aztecs and taking control of their land.

17

Soon after they arrived at the Aztec capital, the Spaniards were at war with the native people. Legend says that during the war, Aztec leaders buried most of the city's treasure in an underground chamber. There is no way to confirm the facts behind this story. But to this day, many Mexicans believe that somewhere under the streets of

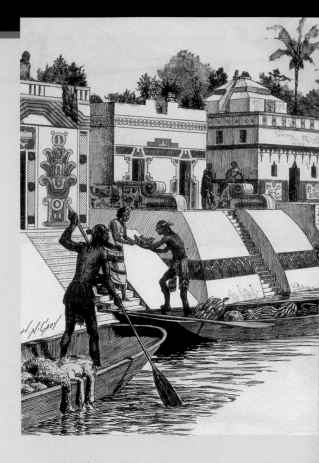

Mexico City lie treasure chests crammed with precious metals and jewels that are worth a fortune.

Ocean in the nation called Peru. A powerful conquistador named Francisco Pizarro wanted to be first to discover and **plunder** this gold-rich land. Pizarro sent ships to explore the Pacific coast of South America. At first, the expeditions found nothing. Then, in 1531, Pizarro set out again, this time accompanied by Hernando de Soto.

De Soto had now been in the Americas for more than 15 years. He was a popular commander who had led men in many battles. A fellow Spaniard described de Soto as "a handsome man, dark in complexion . . . of cheerful **countenance,** an endurer of hardships and very valiant."

Like de Soto, Pizarro came from Extremadura. At first, Pizarro offered de Soto the rank of lieutenant general, which meant he would be second in command. But Pizarro changed his mind and gave his own brother, Hernando Pizarro, the lieutenant general position. De Soto learned that Pizarro was a liar. History records that lying was among the least of Pizarro's crimes.

Still, Hernando de Soto looked forward to

Francisco Pizarro was born in about 1475 in the Extremadura region of Spain. He sailed to the Spanish colony on the island of Hispaniola (which today contains the nations of Haiti and the Dominican Republic) in 1502.

De Soto, Pizarro, and a band of Spanish soldiers marched boldly into the Andes Mountains. The Andes were snowcapped peaks, higher than any peaks the conquistadores had ever seen in Spain. In green valleys, the Spaniards saw herds of curious beasts—llamas—grazing as peacefully as sheep. The conquistadores passed through villages where people greeted them with friendly gifts of food. But not all contact with the Inca people was peaceful. Several times, the Spaniards were attacked by warriors carrying clubs and spears. As usual, Spanish firearms and horses prevailed in battle.

Llamas are native to South America, and they are related to camels. De Soto and Pizarro had never seen llamas before they explored the Andes Mountain region.

In November 1532, the conquistadores arranged a meeting with Atahualpa, ruler of all the Incas. The Inca chief came to the meeting with an army of 3,000 warriors. The Spaniards faced this army with their own force of about 170 men. A Spanish priest handed Atahualpa a Bible. Speaking through an interpreter, the priest told Atahualpa that he was now a subject of the Spanish king and that his people must accept Christianity as their religion.

Atahualpa was the 13th emperor of the Inca.

No doubt the Inca leader was shocked by these foreigners and their demands. In a rage, Atahualpa flung the Bible to the ground. This act triggered a furious battle. Spaniards fired at the Incas. Horsemen rode into the Inca ranks, trampling the warriors and slaying

Spanish missionary Vicente de Valverde speaks to Atahualpa, advising him that he must accept Christianity and become a subject of the king of Spain.

Hoping to win the release of Atahualpa, the Incas filled a room with gold and silver treasures.

them with spears. The battle lasted only half an hour. Thousands of Inca men were killed, and Pizarro captured Atahualpa.

To Pizarro, the Inca chief was a valuable **hostage.** The Spaniards and Atahualpa agreed that Atahualpa would go free if his people filled a room up to the ceiling with gold and other treasures. The demand seemed impossible. Nowhere in the entire world was

Pizarro ordered the murder of Atahualpa, even though the ransom of a roomful of gold and silver was provided.

there a fortune that great. Yet, piece by piece, the demand was met. Common people donated their silver cups. Holy men surrendered beautifully carved gold statues from their temples. The room was soon filled with treasure exactly as Pizarro and Atahualpa had agreed. But Pizarro still ordered his men to kill Atahualpa.

De Soto was outraged by Pizarro's actions. He believed the Spaniards had to keep their promises to the Indian people. Nevertheless, de Soto took his share of the great Inca treasure. He was now a rich man. De Soto sailed back to Spain in 1535. There he married the lovely Isabel. He became one of the most respected men in Spain. Even the Spanish king, Charles V, sought an audience with him. This was quite an honor for a man from Extremadura.

Charles V was born in 1500 in Ghent, Belgium.

Chapter Four

Return to the Americas

In 1539, de Soto led an army of 600 Spanish soldiers into what is now the state of Florida. He hoped to discover great riches, similar to what he and Pizarro found in Peru. Florida, he had heard, was "a land of gold." But de Soto was also moved by an exploring spirit. He hungered to see new lands.

Before de Soto arrived, several Spaniards had touched upon the shores of Florida. The most famous of these was Ponce de Léon, who began a Florida expedition in 1513. Ponce de Léon sought the Fountain of Youth, a magical spring or river. It was said that drinking the waters of this spring could make an old person become young. The spring was a **myth.** No such Fountain of Youth existed anywhere on Earth. Still, in his search, Ponce de Léon explored parts of Florida. It was he who named the region for the

Hernando de Soto and his band of explorers at present-day Tampa Bay, Florida, in 1539.

Easter season and the gorgeous wildflowers he found growing there. In Spanish, the word *florida* means "full of flowers."

De Soto's party landed near present-day Tampa Bay, Florida, in May 1539. True to Spanish rules, de Soto claimed this land for the king of Spain. Spanish priests also told the Indian people that they were now Christians and must worship the Christian God. The Indians turned hostile. Native American warriors

De Soto and his men often used violence against Native Americans as they traveled through Florida seeking riches.

repeatedly attacked de Soto's party and then fled into the thick Florida underbrush.

These hit-and-run raids frustrated de Soto's men. One of his soldiers wrote, "The . . . Indians never remain quiet, but are continually running, traversing from place to place, so that neither crossbow nor arquebus [the Spanish firearm] can be aimed at them. Before a Christian can make a single shot, an Indian will discharge three or four arrows; and he seldom misses a shot."

A museum display shows Spanish soldiers in typical suits of armor. Spanish explorers in the Americas often wore suits of armor as protection against Native American weapons.

Warfare in Florida frustrated de Soto, too. And he found very little gold in this new land. Perhaps the frustration he felt changed his personality. In the past, he had been at least reasonably fair when dealing with Native Americans. Usually he tried to make peace with Indian groups he encountered. In Florida, however, he became quick to wage war.

De Soto ordered his men to march north. He believed the riches of Florida were to be found inland, as was true in Mexico and Peru. Adopting Pizarro's tactics, de Soto entered a village and immediately seized the chief. He then held the chief hostage until the people of the village brought him food and whatever gold jewelry they might possess.

The Spaniards continued their northward advance into what is now the state of Georgia. De Soto's men crossed rivers and swamps. Often they had to build bridges to take horses and supplies over the waters. The heat was oppressive. Mosquitoes tormented the soldiers. The men had to wear iron armor almost constantly because they never knew when the next Indian attack would come. Many soldiers pleaded with their commander to turn back toward the coast, where a fleet waited to take them out of this cursed land. But de Soto ordered them to press forward.

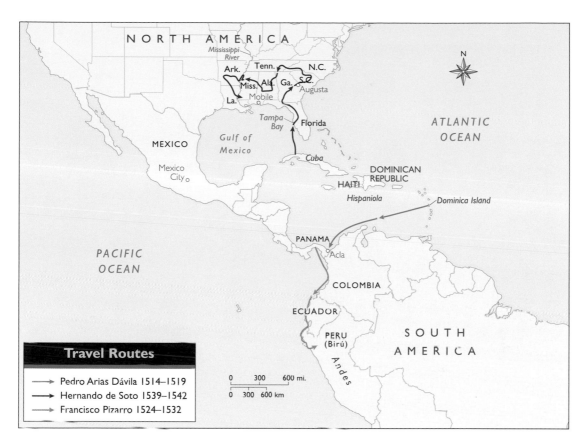

Hernando de Soto was an adventurer who spent many years exploring North America and South America.

Near what is now South Carolina, de Soto's men met a beautiful Indian leader. She was kind to the Spaniards and gave them food. She also gave de Soto a string of exquisite pearls. But he wanted gold. De Soto seized the woman and held her captive. In this way, he forced her tribe to help his men carry supplies. One of his soldiers bitterly wrote, "He [de Soto] would not be content with good land or pearls."

The leader of Cofitachequi was a woman. She gave de Soto a gift of fine pearls, but he wanted gold.

The expedition crossed Georgia and journeyed through South Carolina, North Carolina, Tennessee, and Alabama. Near present-day Mobile, Alabama, de Soto's army fought a terrible battle against Native American warriors. The Spaniards triumphed, but they lost nearly 30 soldiers and many of their horses.

Indian guides told de Soto that to the west was a broad river. The river was called Mississippi, which means "Father of the Waters." The conquistadores, now half starved and their clothes in rags, marched west toward this river. In May 1541, de Soto and his men sighted the mighty Mississippi. This sighting forever gave de Soto his place in history. He is recognized as the first European to see the Mississippi River from its inland banks.

The Mississippi also spelled Hernando de Soto's doom. He crossed the great river and advanced into Arkansas and Louisiana. After many months of exploration, he returned to the Mississippi. In the swamps along the riverbanks, de Soto became feverish. Perhaps he caught a disease called **malaria** from the swarms of mosquitoes that lived in the swamps.

De Soto died on May 21, 1542. His followers weighted down his body, towed it to the middle of the Mississippi

In 1541, Hernando de Soto became the first European to see the Mississippi River from its inland banks.

Hernando de Soto was buried in the Mississippi River in 1542.

River, and let it sink. Hernando de Soto was buried in the Father of the Waters, the great river he had discovered.

Historians today hail de Soto as one of history's greatest explorers. His journey from Florida to the Mississippi River covered more than 2,000 miles (3,219 km) over land never before seen by Europeans. True, he was motivated by gold. But above all, Hernando de Soto had the driving curiosity of a pure explorer. He always wanted to see the land across the next river or beyond the next hill. His life as an explorer was certainly an adventure.

1475?: Francisco Pizarro is born in Trujillo, Spain. Vasco Núñez de Balboa is born in Jérez de los Caballeros, Spain.

1492: Christopher Columbus, sailing on a mission for Spain, discovers land in the Americas.

1500?: Hernando de Soto is born in the Spanish province of Extremadura.

1501: Balboa sails for South America with an expedition from Spain.

1502: Pizarro sails for the Americas.

1513: Balboa is the first European to see the Pacific Ocean.

1514: De Soto sails to the New World on a fleet commanded by Colonel Pedrarias.

1519: The Spanish conquistador Hernando Cortés enters the Aztec capital and discovers great treasure there.

1524: De Soto participates in the conquest of Nicaragua.

1531: Francisco Pizarro and de Soto begin their conquest of the Inca nation in present-day Peru.

1535: De Soto, now a wealthy man, returns to Spain and marries Isabel, the daughter of his old boss Pedrarias.

1539: Leading a force of 600 soldiers, de Soto lands in Florida.

1541: After marching some 2,000 miles (3,219 km) through the American South, de Soto becomes the first European to see the Mississippi River from its inland banks.

1542: De Soto dies of a fever. His body is weighted down and buried in the Mississippi River.

countenance (KOUN-ten-nuhnss) A person's countenance is his appearance or facial expression. Hernando de Soto had a cheerful countenance.

fervently (FUR-vuhnt-lee) To believe fervently is to have particularly strong or intense feelings. The Spaniards fervently believed it was their duty as Christians to bring Christianity to the Indians of the Americas.

hostage (HOSS-tij) A hostage is someone who is held captive in hopes of gaining a ransom. To Pizarro, the Inca chief was a valuable hostage.

malaria (muh-LAIR-ee-uh) Malaria is a disease spread by mosquitoes that is often deadly. De Soto may have been infected with malaria by the swarms of mosquitoes that inhabited the swamps he passed through.

mock (MOK) To mock is to imitate a real act. Young Hernando de Soto probably used wooden swords for mock sword fights with his friends.

myth (MITH) A myth is a story dealing with people and events that is based on tall tales, rather than actual facts. The Fountain of Youth is a myth.

plunder (PLUHN-dur) To plunder is to steal on a grand scale. A powerful conquistador named Francisco Pizarro wanted to be first to discover and plunder the gold-rich land of Peru.

scourge (SKURJ) A scourge is something that causes great distress or harm. De Soto learned why Pedrarias was called the Scourge of God.

treason (TREE-zuhn) Treason is the crime of betraying one's own country. In 1519, Pedrarias falsely accused Balboa of treason against the Spanish government.

trekked (TREKT) People who have trekked have walked or marched with determination. De Soto joined an exploring mission that trekked through the wilds of Panama.

Books

Gaines, Ann Graham. *Hernando de Soto and the Spanish Search for Gold in World History.* Berkeley Heights, N.J.: Enslow Publishers, 2002.

Gibbons, Faye, and Bruce Dupree (illustrator). *Hernando de Soto: A Search for Gold and Glory.* Birmingham, Ala.: Crane Hill Publishers, 2002.

Hinds, Kathryn. *The Incas.* New York: Benchmark Books, 1998.

Web Sites

Visit our home page for lots of links about Hernando de Soto:

http://www.childsworld.com/links.html

Note to Parents, Teachers, and Librarians:
We routinely check our Web links to make sure they're safe, active sites—so encourage your readers to check them out!

About the Author

R. Conrad Stein was born in Chicago. At age 18, he joined the Marine Corps and served for three years. He later attended the University of Illinois, where he graduated with a degree in history. A full-time writer, Mr. Stein has published more than 100 books for young readers. He lived in Mexico for many years, and his family still vacations in that country. The author now lives in Chicago with his wife (children's book author Deborah Kent) and their daughter, Janna.

Index

Alabama, 34
Andes Mountains, *20*, 21, 22, *22*
Arias de Ávila, Pedro, 10–11, 12, 14, 15, 20
Atahualpa (Inca ruler), 23, *23*, *24*, 25, *26*, 27
Aztec culture, 17, *17*, 18

de Balboa, Vasco Núñez, 14–15, *15*

Charles V, king of Spain, 27, *27*
Christianity, 12–13, 23, *24*, 29
Colombia, 13–14
Columbus, Christopher, 9, *9*
conquistadores, 6–7, 12–13, 14, 22, *31*, 32
Cortés, Hernando, 17, *17*
Cuzco, Peru, *20*

Dominica, 12, *13*

Extremadura region (Spain), 6, 7, 8, 15, 19

Florida, 28–29, *29*, 32
Fountain of Youth, 28

Georgia, 32
gold, 10, 13, 16, 17, 25, *25*, 27, 32, 33, 36
guns, 14, 22, 30

Hispaniola, 9
horses, 14, 22, 32, 34

Inca Empire, *20*, 21, 22, 23, *23*, *24*, 25, *25*, *26*, 27

Indies, 9

de Léon, Ponce, 28–29
llamas, 22, *22*

Machu Picchu, *20*
malaria, 35
map, *33*
Mississippi River, 34, *35*, *36*
Mobile, Alabama, 34

Native Americans, 6, 7, 9, 12–13, 14, *14*, 29–30, *30*, 32, 33, *34*. *See also* Aztec culture; Inca Empire.

Panama, 16
Pedrarias. *See* Arias de Ávila, Pedro.
Peru, 16, 18, 20, *20*, 21
Pizarro, Francisco, 18, 19, *19*, 25, 27
Pizarro, Hernando, 19

Seville, Spain, 8, 10, *10*
soldiers. *See* conquistadores.
de Soto, Hernando, *8*, *21*, *29*, *30*, *34*, *35*, *36*
    birth, 8
    childhood, 8
    death, 35–36, *36*
    education, 8
    marriage, 20, *21*, 27
South Carolina, 33

Tampa Bay, Florida, 29, *29*

de Valverde, Vincente, *24*